Yankeeology
Trivia
Challenge

New York Yankees Baseball

Yankeeology Trivia Challenge

New York Yankees Baseball

Researched by Tom P. Rippey III

Tom P. Rippey III & Paul F. Wilson, Editors

Kick The Ball, Ltd

Lewis Center, Ohio

Trivia by Kick The Ball, Ltd

College Football Trivia

Alabama Crimson Tide	Auburn Tigers	Boston College Eagles	Florida Gators
Georgia Bulldogs	LSU Tigers	Miami Hurricanes	Michigan Wolverines
Nebraska Cornhuskers	Notre Dame Fighting Irish	Ohio State Buckeyes	Oklahoma Sooners
Oregon Ducks	Penn State Nittany Lions	Southern Cal Trojans	Texas Longhorns

Pro Football Trivia

Arizona Cardinals	Buffalo Bills	Chicago Bears	Cleveland Browns
Denver Broncos	Green Bay Packers	Indianapolis Colts	Kansas City Chiefs
Minnesota Vikings	New England Patriots	Oakland Raiders	Pittsburgh Steelers
San Francisco 49ers	Washington Redskins		

Pro Baseball Trivia

Boston Red Sox	Chicago Cubs	Chicago White Sox	Cincinnati Reds
Detroit Tigers	Los Angeles Dodgers	New York Mets	New York Yankees
Philadelphia Phillies	Saint Louis Cardinals	San Francisco Giants	

College Basketball Trivia

Duke Blue Devils	Georgetown Hoyas	Indiana Hoosiers	Kansas Jayhawks
Kentucky Wildcats	Maryland Terrapins	Michigan State Spartans	North Carolina Tar Heels
Syracuse Orange	UConn Huskies	UCLA Bruins	

Pro Basketball Trivia

Boston Celtics	Chicago Bulls	Detroit Pistons	Los Angeles Lakers
Utah Jazz			

Visit **www.TriviaGameBooks.com** for more details.

This book is dedicated to our families and friends for your unwavering love, support, and your understanding of our pursuit of our passions. Thank you for everything you do for us and for making our lives complete.

Yankeeology Trivia Challenge: New York Yankees Baseball;
Second Edition 2010

Published by
Kick The Ball, Ltd
8595 Columbus Pike, Suite 197
Lewis Center, OH 43035
www.TriviaGameBooks.com

Designed, Formatted, and Edited by: Tom P. Rippey III & Paul F. Wilson
Researched by: Tom P. Rippey III

For information on ordering this book in bulk at reduced prices, please email us
at pfwilson@triviagamebooks.com.

International Standard Book Number: 978-1-934372-78-4

Printed and Bound in the United States of America

10 9 8 7 6 5 4 3 2 1

Table of Contents

Dear Friend,

Thank you for purchasing our *Yankeeology Trivia Challenge* game book!

We have made every attempt to verify the accuracy of the questions and answers contained in this book. However it is still possible that from time to time an error has been made by us or our researchers. In the event you find a question or answer that is questionable or inaccurate, we ask for your understanding and thank you for bringing it to our attention so we may improve future editions of this book. Please email us at tprippey@triviagamebooks.com with those observations and comments.

Have fun playing *Yankeeology Trivia Challenge*!

Tom and Paul

Tom Rippey and Paul Wilson
Co-Founders, Kick The Ball, Ltd

PS – You can discover more about all of our current trivia game books by visiting www.TriviaGameBooks.com.

Book Format:

There are four quarters, each made up of fifty questions. Each quarter's questions have assigned point values. Questions are designed to get progressively more difficult as you proceed through each quarter, as well as through the book itself. Most questions are in a four-option multiple-choice format so that you will at least have a 25% chance of getting a correct answer for some of the more challenging questions.

We have even added extra innings in the event of a tie, or just in case you want to keep playing a little longer.

Game Options:

One Player -
To play on your own, simply answer each of the questions in all the quarters, and in the overtime section, if you'd like. Use the Player / Team Score Sheet to record your answers and the quarter Answer Keys to check your answers. Calculate each quarter's points and the total for the game at the bottom of the Player / Team Score Sheet to determine your final score.

Two or More Players –
To play with multiple players decide if you will all be competing with each other individually, or if you will form and play as teams. Each player / team will then have its own Player / Team Score Sheet to record its answer. You can use the quarter Answer Keys to check your answers and to calculate your final scores.

The Player / Team Score Sheets have been designed so that each team can answer all questions or you can divide the questions up in any combination you would prefer. For example, you may want to alternate questions if two players are playing or answer every third question for three players, etc. In any case, simply record your response to your questions in the corresponding quarter and question number on the Player / Team Score Sheet.

A winner will be determined by multiplying the total number of correct answers for each quarter by the point value per quarter, then adding together the final total for all quarters combined. Play the game again and again by alternating the questions that your team is assigned so that you will answer a different set of questions each time you play.

You Create the Game -
There are countless other ways of using *Yankeeology Trivia Challenge* questions. It is limited only to your imagination. Examples might be using them at your tailgate or other professional baseball related party. Players / Teams who answer questions incorrectly may have to perform a required action, or winners may receive special prizes. Let us know what other games you come up with!

Have fun!

1) When was the nickname Yankees officially adopted by New York?

Answers begin on page 17

   A) 1908
   B) 1913
   C) 1919
   D) 1922

2) What are the Yankees' official colors?

   A) Gray and Blue
   B) Black and Gray
   C) Black and Navy
   D) Navy and White

3) New York's stadium has a seating capacity over 70,000.

   A) True
   B) False

4) What year did the Yankees play their first-ever game?

   A) 1890
   B) 1897
   C) 1903
   D) 1912

5) From which team did the Yankees buy Babe Ruth's contract?

    A)   Brooklyn Robins
    B)   New York Giants
    C)   Chicago White Sox
    D)   Boston Red Sox

6) In which American League division do the Yankees play?

    A)   Central
    B)   East
    C)   West
    D)   Northeast

7) Did the Yankees win greater than 95 games in the 2009 regular season?

    A)   Yes
    B)   No

8) Who had the longest tenure managing the Yankees?

    A)   Joe Torre
    B)   Bob Lemon
    C)   Billy Martin
    D)   Joe McCarthy

9) Was Derek Jeter drafted by the Yankees?

    A) Yes
    B) No

10) What was the original purchase price of the Yankees?

    A) $18,000
    B) $25,000
    C) $28,500
    D) $30, 900

11) Who was the Yankees' opponent in their most recent World Series appearance?

    A) Atlanta Braves
    B) Florida Marlins
    C) Philadelphia Phillies
    D) Cincinnati Reds

12) The Yankees won the American League Pennant greater than 50 times.

    A) True
    B) False

13) What was the nickname given to the 1927 Yankees team?

   A) Back Wall Busters
   B) Bat Breakers
   C) Murderers Row
   D) Ball Murderers

14) Don Larson is the only player in MLB history to pitch a perfect game in the World Series.

   A) True
   B) False

15) What is the name of the Yankees' home stadium?

   A) New York Ball Park
   B) Yankee Stadium
   C) Liberty Field
   D) Ruth Field

16) Who is the Yankees' current manager?

   A) Joe Torre
   B) Don Mattingly
   C) Joe Girardi
   D) Bucky Dent

17) Who did the Yankees play in the 2009 American League Divisional Series?

    A) Detroit Tigers
    B) Baltimore Orioles
    C) Boston Red Sox
    D) Minnesota Twins

18) What season did the Yankees play in their first-ever World Series?

    A) 1918
    B) 1921
    C) 1925
    D) 1929

19) Who holds the Yankees' career record for games pitched?

    A) Mariano Rivera
    B) Whitey Ford
    C) Ron Guidry
    D) Andy Pettitte

20) Who hit the most home runs for the Yankees in 2009?

    A) Dere Jeter
    B) Mark Teixeira
    C) Hideki Matsui
    D) Alex Rodriguez

21) How many years did the Yankees share a ballpark with the New York Giants?

    A) 4
    B) 7
    C) 10
    D) 14

22) How many all-time World Series have the Yankees won?

    A) 19
    B) 21
    C) 24
    D) 27

23) How many total runs did the Yankees score in 2009?

    A) 822
    B) 860
    C) 915
    D) 968

24) How many seasons have the Yankees won 100 or more games?

    A) 12
    B) 16
    C) 19
    D) 23

25) How many Yankees players have been named American League Most Valuable Player?

   A) 11
   B) 13
   C) 17
   D) 19

26) What nickname did New York go by before Yankees?

   A) Highlanders
   B) Warriors
   C) Slammers
   D) Bombers

27) Did the Yankees have a winning record at the midseason break in 2009?

   A) Yes
   B) No

28) What is the name of the area behind center field at Yankee Stadium?

   A) Yankee Hall
   B) Pinstripe Cove
   C) Player Central
   D) Monument Park

29) Was Yogi Berra selected as an All-Star every year he played for the Yankees?

    A) Yes
    B) No

30) What season did Lou Gehrig give his farewell address?

    A) 1935
    B) 1939
    C) 1941
    D) 1943

31) How many times has a Yankees pitcher won 20 or more games in a season?

    A) 42
    B) 51
    C) 58
    D) 64

32) When was the last time the Yankees lost greater than 100 games in a season?

    A) 1912
    B) 1944
    C) 1960
    D) 1987

33) What was the original distance to the center field wall at Yankee Stadium?

   A) 401'
   B) 434'
   C) 467'
   D) 490'

34) What is the Yankees' record for consecutive games with a safe hit?

   A) 45
   B) 50
   C) 56
   D) 64

35) Who was the most recent Yankee to win a Cy Young Award?

   A) Mike Mussina
   B) Andy Pettitte
   C) Roger Clemens
   D) David Wells

36) Which Yankees pitcher had the most wins in the regular season in 2009?

   A) Andy Pettitte
   B) CC Sabathia
   C) Joba Chamberlain
   D) A.J. Burnett

37) Who is the only Yankee to hit four home runs in the same game?

    A) Reggie Jackson
    B) Babe Ruth
    C) Greg Nettles
    D) Lou Gehrig

38) Against which AL team did the Yankees have the highest winning percentage during the 2009 regular season?

    A) Texas Rangers
    B) Minnesota Twins
    C) Baltimore Orioles
    D) Cleveland Indians

39) What season did the Yankees first win the World Series?

    A) 1923
    B) 1926
    C) 1928
    D) 1931

40) What was Joe DiMaggio's nickname while playing for the Yankees?

    A) Yankee Clipper
    B) Italian Bomber
    C) Home Run Joe
    D) Mr. Dependable

41) Which Yankee had the most RBIs in the 2009 World Series?

    A) Derek Jeter
    B) Jorge Posada
    C) Hideki Matsui
    D) Alex Rodriguez

42) How many times have the Yankees scored greater than 1,000 runs in a season?

    A) 0
    B) 2
    C) 4
    D) 7

43) Which of the following pitchers did not throw a perfect game as a Yankee?

    A) Ron Guidry
    B) David Wells
    C) Don Larson
    D) David Cone

44) How many Yankees were selected to the 2009 All-Star Game?

    A) 1
    B) 3
    C) 4
    D) 6

45) Which Yankees player holds the record for most grand slams in a career?

    A)   Roger Maris
    B)   Joe DiMaggio
    C)   Bernie Williams
    D)   Lou Gehrig

46) What are the most Yankees selected as All-Stars in a single season?

    A)   4
    B)   7
    C)   9
    D)   11

47) How many Yankees managers lasted one season or less?

    A)   2
    B)   6
    C)   8
    D)   10

48) How many hits did the Yankees pitching staff have in the 2009 regular season?

    A)   1
    B)   3
    C)   4
    D)   7

49) What is the nickname of the AAA team affiliated with the Yankees?

   A)   Scranton/Wilkes-Barre Yankees
   B)   Columbus Clippers
   C)   Charleston RiverDogs
   D)   Trenton Thunder

50) When was the first-ever season the Yankees had a winning record against the Red Sox?

   A)   1903
   B)   1906
   C)   1912
   D)   1915

One of the most recognizable sports logos in the world is the interlocking N and Y of the New York Yankees. The first use of the logo was not for the Yankees or any other sports team for that matter. It was designed by Louis B. Tiffany in 1877 as a medal for New York City police officer John McDowell, the first city police officer shot in the line of duty. Yankee owner Bill Devery, a former NYC police chief, may have been the driving force in introducing the logo to the Yankees uniform. Interestingly the logo was removed from the jersey from 1917-36. One of the greatest players to ever put on a Yankees uniform, Babe Ruth, never wore a jersey with the interlocking NY insignia.

1) B – 1913 (Some newspapers referred to the team as the Yankees as early as 1905.)
2) D – Navy and White
3) B – False (The current stadium has a seating capacity of 50,235 and an overall capacity of 52,325 with standing room only included.)
4) C – 1903 (A 3-1 loss to the Washington Senators)
5) D – Boston Red Sox (The Yankees bought Ruth's contract in 1919. In return, New York gave Boston $125,000 and a $350,000 loan.)
6) B – East (Along with Toronto Blue Jays, Boston Red Sox, Baltimore Orioles, and Tampa Bay Rays)
7) A – Yes (The Yankees finished the season with a record of 103-59.)
8) D – Joe McCarthy (16 years, 1931-46)
9) A – Yes (Derek was the Yankees' first pick [6th overall], in the 1992 draft out of Kalamazoo Central H.S. [Michigan].)
10) A – $18,000 (The Baltimore Orioles franchise folded in 1903. Bill Devery and Frank Farrell bought the franchise and moved it to New York.)
11) C – Philadelphia Phillies (The Yankees won the series 4-2 against the Philadelphia Phillies in 2009.)

12) B – False (The Yankees have won the AL Pennant 40 times, the last one in 2009.)

13) C – Murderers Row (Babe Ruth led the team with a then-league record 60 home runs.)

14) A – True (The Yankees beat the Brooklyn Dodgers 2-0 in game five and went on to win the World Series.)

15) B – Yankee Stadium (Opened in 2009 with a construction cost of $1.5 billion dollars. The original Yankee Stadium had a construction cost of $2.5 million in 1923 [$31.6 million adjusted for inflation].)

16) C – Joe Girardi (Joe has managed the Yankees since 2008.)

17) D – Minnesota Twins (The Yankees swept the Twins 3-0.)

18) B – 1921 (The Yankees played the New York Giants with whom they shared a ballpark. The Giants went on to win the series 5-3.)

19) A – Mariano Rivera (Mariano has pitched in a total of 917 games as a Yankee.)

20) B – Mark Teixeira (He led the team with 39 home runs in 2009, his first season as a Yankee.)

21) C – 10 (The Yankees were invited by the Giants to share the Polo Grounds in 1913. They played there until Yankee Stadium opened in 1923.)

22) D – 27 (Most recently in 2009 when the Yankees defeated the Phillies 4-2.)

23) C – 915 (This was the most in the entire league. The Angels were second with 883 runs scored.)

24) C – 19 (The last time was in 2009 [103 wins].)

25) B – 13 (The most recent Yankee to receive the award was Alex Rodriguez in 2007.)

26) A – Highlanders (This was from 1903-12, stemming from the fact that the Yankees' ballpark was at one of the highest points in Manhattan. Hilltop Park was located at 168th St. and Broadway.)

27) A – Yes (New York had a record of 51-37 [.580].)

28) D – Monument Park (There are five monuments honoring Yankees greats [Miller Huggins, Lou Gehrig, Babe Ruth, Mickey Mantle, and Joe DiMaggio] and a sixth to honor those fallen in the 9/11 attacks. There are also many plaques dedicated to other players and those who have dedicated themselves to the Yankees organization.)

29) B – No (It was close, though. Berra played for the Yankees from 1946-63 and was an All-Star selection from 1948-62.)

30) B – 1939 (A special "Lou Gehrig Appreciation Day" was held at Yankee Stadium on July 4, 1969, for over 62,000 fans.)

31) C – 58 (The most recent pitcher to have 20 wins in a season for the Yankees was Mike Mussina in 2008 [20-9].)

32) A – 1912 (New York went 50-102. The only other time the Yankees lost more than 100 games in a season was 1908 when they finished 51-103.)

33) D – 490' (This was decreased to 461' in 1937 due to expansion of the stadium.)

34) C – 56 (Joe DiMaggio accomplished this feat in 1941 and it still stands as the league record. The NL record is 48 set by Willie Keeler in 1897.)

35) C – Roger Clemens (He was awarded the AL Cy Young Award in 2001, with a 20-3 record and 3.51 ERA.)

36) B – CC Sabathia (Sabathia finished the regular season with a 19-8 record.)

37) D – Lou Gehrig (Gehrig hit a franchise-high four home runs against Philadelphia in 1932.)

38) B – Minnesota Twins (New York swept the Twins both series during the regular season for a 7-0 record.)

39) A – 1923 (The Yankees beat the New York Giants 4-2 in the World Series. This was also their first year in Yankee Stadium.)

40) A – Yankee Clipper (Joe played a total of 14 seasons with the Yankees. They only missed the World Series three of those seasons [1940, 1946, and 1948].)

41) C – Hideki Matsui (Hideki had 8 hits and drove in 8 runs in the World Series. He tied a single-game World Series record with six RBIs in Game Six.)

42) C – 4 (1,062 runs in 1930, 1,067 runs in 1931, 1,002 runs in 1932, and 1,065 runs in 1936)

43) A – Ron Guidry (The Yankees have had three pitchers toss a perfect game, Don Larson in 1956, David Wells in 1998, and David Cone in 1999.)

44) B – 3 (Derek Jeter, Mark Teixeira, and Mariano Rivera)

45) D – Lou Gehrig (Gehrig hit 23 grand slams in his career, which is also the MLB record.)

46) C – 9 (The Yankees have had nine players selected as All-Stars on five different occasions [1939, 1942, 1947, 1958, and 1959].)

47) D – 10 (The last manager to last just one season was Dallas Green in 1989.)

48) B – 3 (The pitching staff had 24 at-bats for a combined total of three hits [.125 on-base percentage].)

49) A – Scranton/Wilkes-Barre Yankees (They have been affiliated with New York since 2007.)

50) B – 1906 (The Yankees were 17-5 versus Boston that season.)

Note: All answers valid as of the end of the 2009 season, unless otherwise indicated in the question itself.

1) What year did pinstripes first appear on Yankees uniforms?

Answers begin on page 37

   A)   1909
   B)   1912
   C)   1921
   D)   1928

2) What jersey number did Yankees great Babe Ruth wear?

   A)   #3
   B)   #7
   C)   #12
   D)   #23

3) Not including 2010 inductees, how many players have been inducted into the National Baseball Hall of Fame with the Yankees as their primary team?

   A)   15
   B)   19
   C)   22
   D)   25

4) Where did the Yankees play from 1974-75 while the old Yankee Stadium was being renovated?

   A)   Meadowlands
   B)   Carrier Dome
   C)   Shea Stadium
   D)   Rutgers Stadium

5) Did the Yankees have a winning record on the road during the 2009 regular season?

    A) Yes
    B) No

6) How many times did New York sweep a series during the 2009 regular season?

    A) 5
    B) 8
    C) 10
    D) 13

7) Who broke Babe Ruth's MLB single-season home run record?

    A) Mickey Mantle
    B) Roger Maris
    C) Alex Rodriguez
    D) Joe DiMaggio

8) All of the following Yankees players were named AL Most Valuable Player three times, except?

    A) Lou Gehrig
    B) Yogi Berra
    C) Joe DiMaggio
    D) Mickey Mantle

9) The Yankees' Whitey Ford was a right-handed pitcher.

    A) True
    B) False

10) Which American League opponent have the Yankees played fewer than 400 times in the regular season?

    A) Toronto Blue Jays
    B) Los Angeles Angles of Anaheim
    C) Texas Rangers
    D) Seattle Mariners

11) What is New York's all-time regular-season winning percentage against the Red Sox?

    A) .468
    B) .498
    C) .528
    D) .550

12) Since 1969, who is the only Yankees pitcher to lead the league in saves for greater than three seasons?

    A) Dave Righetti
    B) Sparky Lyle
    C) Mariano Rivera
    D) Rich Gossage

13) How many times have Yankees pitchers been awarded the Cy Young Award?

    A) 2
    B) 5
    C) 7
    D) 10

14) What year was New York's first-ever winning season?

    A) 1903
    B) 1906
    C) 1910
    D) 1912

15) What is the Yankees' record for most hits as a team in a single season?

    A) 1,560
    B) 1,631
    C) 1,683
    D) 1,722

16) Who holds the Yankees' record for most grand slams in a season?

    A) Don Mattingly
    B) Alex Rodriguez
    C) Mickey Mantle
    D) Babe Ruth

17) What is the Yankees' record for fewest errors in a season?

A) 52
B) 61
C) 69
D) 83

18) Which Yankees pitcher had the lowest ERA in 2009 (minimum 50 innings pitched)?

A) Phil Coke
B) Mariano Rivera
C) Philip Hughes
D) CC Sabathia

19) How many Yankees players have been walked greater than 150 times in a single season?

A) 1
B) 3
C) 4
D) 6

20) The Yankees have won greater than 10,000 all-time regular-season games.

A) True
B) False

21) Which team have the Yankees played the greatest number of times in the World Series?

    A) San Francisco Giants
    B) Cincinnati Reds
    C) Los Angeles Dodgers
    D) Atlanta Braves

22) Which Yankees player had the highest fielding percentage in 2009 (minimum 100 games played)?

    A) Johnny Damon
    B) Melky Cabrera
    C) Derek Jeter
    D) Mark Teixeira

23) What was the highest single-season salary paid to Babe Ruth by the Yankees?

    A) $50,000
    B) $65,000
    C) $80,000
    D) $98,000

24) When was the last time the Yankees had two Gold Glove Award winners in the same season?

    A) 1997
    B) 2000
    C) 2006
    D) 2009

25) Who was New York's manager their first-ever season?

A) Hal Chase
B) Clark Griffith
C) William Donovan
D) George Stallings

26) Who is the Yankees' current team captain?

A) Alex Rodriguez
B) Johnny Damon
C) Mariano Rivera
D) Derek Jeter

27) What is the nickname of the series between the Yankees and the Mets?

A) Brooklyn Bridge Series
B) Central Park Series
C) Subway Series
D) Liberty Series

28) Who is the only Yankee to be named All-Star MVP?

A) Derek Jeter
B) Don Mattingly
C) Reggie Jackson
D) Roger Maris

29) When was the last time a Yankees player won the American League batting title?

    A) 1995
    B) 1998
    C) 2002
    D) 2006

30) How many teams had a winning record against New York in the Yankees' first-ever season?

    A) 1
    B) 3
    C) 5
    D) 7

31) Who is the only Yankees player to win the World Series MVP Award on a losing team?

    A) Bobby Richardson
    B) Wade Boggs
    C) Don Mattingly
    D) Joe DiMaggio

32) Against which American League team does New York have the highest all-time winning percentage (min. 500 games played)?

    A) Minnesota Twins
    B) Boston Red Sox
    C) Baltimore Orioles
    D) Los Angeles Angels of Anaheim

33) Who holds the Yankees' record for most strikeouts in a single game?

    A) Andy Pettitte
    B) Whitey Ford
    C) Ron Guidry
    D) David Cone

34) Which season did the Yankees first play the Red Sox in the postseason?

    A) 1978
    B) 1983
    C) 1992
    D) 1999

35) What are the most runs ever allowed by the Yankees in a single game?

    A) 18
    B) 21
    C) 24
    D) 28

36) Lou Gehrig had more seasons with 200 or more hits than Babe Ruth and Joe DiMaggio combined.

    A) True
    B) False

37) Who was New York's first-ever opponent in Yankee Stadium?

    A) Chicago White Sox
    B) Boston Red Sox
    C) Detroit Tigers
    D) Baltimore Orioles

38) How many times has a Yankee hit for the cycle (single, double, triple, and home run in the same game)?

    A) 7
    B) 10
    C) 12
    D) 15

39) Which Yankees pitcher holds New York's record for the lowest ERA in a season?

    A) Jack Chesbro
    B) Roger Clemens
    C) Spud Chandler
    D) Ron Guidry

40) Has any Yankees player ever had a batting average of .400 or higher for a single season?

    A) Yes
    B) No

41) Who holds the Yankees' career record for stolen bases?

    A) Rickey Henderson
    B) Bernie Williams
    C) Derek Jeter
    D) Ben Chapman

42) How many players have played 2,000 or more games as a Yankee?

    A) 3
    B) 6
    C) 8
    D) 11

43) What is the nickname of the AA team associated with New York?

    A) Tampa Yankees
    B) GCL Yankees
    C) Trenton Thunder
    D) Charleston RiverDogs

44) How many times have the Yankees been swept in the World Series?

    A) 1
    B) 3
    C) 4
    D) 6

45) Who was the only Yankee to wear jersey #4?

    A)   Joe DiMaggio
    B)   Mickey Mantle
    C)   Yogi Berra
    D)   Lou Gehrig

46) When did the Yankees last host the All-Star Game?

    A)   1939
    B)   1960
    C)   1977
    D)   2008

47) How many Yankees players have their jersey number retired?

    A)   9
    B)   13
    C)   15
    D)   18

48) How many times did Joe Torre win American League Manager of the Year as a Yankee?

    A)   1
    B)   2
    C)   4
    D)   5

49) What decade did the Yankees have the highest winning percentage during the regular season?

    A) 1930s
    B) 1950s
    C) 1980s
    D) 2000s

50) How many Yankees have won the World Series MVP Award?

    A) 6
    B) 8
    C) 10
    D) 12

Longtime Yankee Stadium public address announcer, Bob Sheppard, was considered The Voice of Yankee Stadium for many years. Sheppard worked his first game as the PA announcer in 1951. He would go on to work over 4,500 Yankees games in his distinguished career. When not working the booth, he made many cameo appearances in movies and television shows, gave eulogies for many of our nation's icons (including former President Ronald Regan), and even threw out the first pitch for a World Series game, just to name a few of his many extra-curricular activities. In 2009 at age 99, he officially announced his intention to retire following the season. Not surprisingly, the Yankees renamed their media dining room "Sheppard's Place" in his honor. What is surprising, however, is that all of this almost never happened because he initially turned down the job due to scheduling conflicts with his original profession – he was a high school speech teacher.

1) B – 1912 (They first appeared on opening day that season, but were removed during the 1913 and 1914 seasons.)

2) A – #3 (Babe played for the Yankees from 1920-34. His jersey number was retired in 1948. Cliff Mapes was the last Yankee to wear #3.)

3) B – 19 (The last inductee was Joe "Flash" Gordon in 2009. Sixteen other players, who played at least one season with the Yankees, are inducted for other primary teams.)

4) C – Shea Stadium (They had an overall record of 172-150 [.534] while sharing the Mets' home field.)

5) A – Yes (New York went 46-35 on the road for a .568 winning percentage.)

6) D – 13 (The Yankees had regular-season series records of 2-0 against the A's and Blue Jays; 3-0 against the Orioles [3 series], Mets, Twins, Tigers, White Sox, and Red Sox; and 4-0 against the Twins, Red Sox, and Rays.)

7) B – Roger Maris (Maris broke Ruth's home-run record in the fourth inning of the last game of the 1961 regular season.)

8) A – Lou Gehrig (Gehrig won two MVP awards, the first in 1927 and the second in 1936. Joe DiMaggio, Yogi Berra, and Mickey Mantle are the only Yankees to win three.)

9) B – False (His career record of 236-106 made him the winningest left-handed pitcher in the 20th Century.)

10) D – Seattle Mariners (The Yankees have an overall record of 197-157 [.556] against Seattle. The only other current AL team New York has played fewer than 400 times is Tampa Bay [132-68, .660].)

11) D – .550 (The Yankees have an overall regular-season record of 1,104-908 [.548] against the Red Sox.)

12) C – Mariano Rivera (He led the league in saves in 1999 [45], 2001 [50], and 2004 [53]. Saves became an official statistic in 1969 and the only other Yankees to lead the league in saves are Rich Gossage [1978 and 1980] and Dave Righetti [1986].)

13) B – 5 (Bob Turley [1958], Whitey Ford [1961], Sparky Lyle [1977], Ron Guidry [1978], and Roger Clemens [2001])

14) A – 1903 (72-62 [.537] record their inaugural season)

15) C – 1,683 (This NY record has held up since 1930.)

16) A – Don Mattingly (Don hit all six of his career grand slams in just one season [1987].)

17) D – 83 (This was set in 2008.)

18) B – Mariano Rivera (1.76 ERA through 66.1 innings.)

19) A – 1 (Babe Ruth was walked 170 times in 1923. This is still an AL single-season record.)

20) B – False (NY's all-time record for the regular season is 9,457-7,141 for a .570 winning percentage.)

21) C – Los Angeles Dodgers (The Yankees played the Dodgers 11 times in the World Series [1941, 1947, 1949, 1952, 1953, 1955, 1956, 1963, 1977, 1978, and 1981]. The Yankees won 8 of them.)

22) D – Mark Teixeira (He recorded 1,222 putouts with 49 assists and only four errors, for a fielding percentage of .997.)

23) C – $80,000 (That is equivalent to just over $1 million in 2009. ARod was paid over $33 million in 2009.)

24) D – 2009 (Derek Jeter won his 4th Gold Glove [2004-06, and 2009] and Mark Teixeira won his 1st as a Yankee, but 3rd overall [2005, 2006, and 2009].)

25) B – Clark Griffith (He managed New York from 1903-08 with a combined record of 419-370 [.531].)

26) D – Derek Jeter (Derek has held the position of team captain since 2003.)

27) C – Subway Series (This term was also used to describe the match-ups between the Yankees and either one of their NL opponents, New York Giants or Brooklyn Dodgers, before both left the city at the end of 1957.)

28) A – Derek Jeter (All-Star MVPs were not named until 1962. He is the only Yankee to win one [2000].)

29) B – 1998 (Bernie Williams won the title with a .339 batting average.)

30) B – 3 (New York had losing records to the Red Sox [7-13], Indians [6-14], and Tigers [9-10].)

31) A – Bobby Richardson (In the 1960 WS against the Pirates, Bobby had a .367 batting average with 12 RBIs and only 1 strikeout over the 7 game series. He is the only major league player to win the award on a losing team.)

32) C – Baltimore Orioles (The Yankees have an all-time regular-season record of 1,208-813 against Baltimore, for a .598 winning percentage.)

33) C – Ron Guidry (He struck out 18 Angels in 1978.)

34) D – 1999 (The Yankees beat the Red Sox 4-1 in the ALCS, before going on to win the World Series.)

35) C – 24 (The Yankees lost 6-24 at Cleveland Indians on July 29, 1928.)

36) A – True (Gehrig had nine seasons with 200 or more hits [1927, 1928, 1930-34, 1936, and 1937]. Babe Ruth [1921, 1923, and 1924] and Joe DiMaggio [1936 and 1937] combined for 5 seasons.)

37) B – Boston Red Sox (The Yankees recorded a 4-1 win over Boston in their first game in Yankee Stadium.)

38) D – 15 (Most recently by Melky Cabrera in 2009.)

39) C – Spud Chandler (Spud set this record in 1943 with a 1.64 ERA, while compiling a 20-4 record. His ERA and total wins were also league highs that year.)

40) B – No (Babe Ruth was closest, .393 average in 1923.)

41) A – Rickey Henderson (Rickey stole 326 bases during his career as a Yankee [1985-1989].)

42) B – 6 (Mickey Mantle [2,401], Lou Gehrig [2,164], Derek Jeter [2138], Yogi Berra [2,116], Babe Ruth [2,084], and Bernie Williams [2,076])

43) C – Trenton Thunder (The Trenton Thunder play in Trenton, N.J. and have been affiliated with the Yankees since 2003.)

44) B – 3 (The Yankees were swept by the Giants in 1922, Dodgers in 1963, and Reds in 1976.)

45) D – Lou Gehrig (Gehrig was a Yankee from 1929-39. His jersey number was retired upon his retirement.)

46) D – 2008 (The Yankees also hosted the All-Star Game in 1939, 1960, and 1977. The AL is 1-3 at Yankee Stadium, with their only win in 1939.)

47) C – 15 (Billy Martin [#1], Babe Ruth [#3], Lou Gehrig [#4], Joe DiMaggio [#5], Mickey Mantle [#7], Yogi Berra [#8], Bill Dickey [#8], Roger Maris [#9], Phil Rizzuto [#10], Thurman Munson [#15], Whitey Ford [#16], Don Mattingly [#23], Elston Howard [#32], Reggie Jackson [#44], and Ron Guidry [#49])

48) B – 2 (Joe won this award in 1996 and 1998.)

49) A – 1930s (New York had an overall record of 970-554, for a .636 winning percentage.)

50) D – 12 (Don Larson [1956], Bob Turley [1958], Bobby Richardson [1960], Whitey Ford [1961], Ralph Terry [1962], Reggie Jackson [1977], Bucky Dent [1978], John Wetteland [1996], Scott Brosius [1998], Mariano Rivera [1999], Derek Jeter [2000], and Hideki Matsui [2009])

Note: All answers valid as of the end of the 2009 season, unless otherwise indicated in the question itself.

1) How many career grand slams has Derek Jeter hit for the Yankees?

Answers begin on page 56

   A) 1
   B) 3
   C) 4
   D) 5

2) Who hit the first home run in the current Yankee Stadium?

   A) Hideki Matsui
   B) Melky Cabrera
   C) Jorge Posada
   D) Alex Rodriguez

3) When was the most recent season the Yankees failed to go .500?

   A) 1961
   B) 1972
   C) 1980
   D) 1992

4) Which Yankees manager has the second most career wins?

   A) Casey Stengel
   B) Joe Torre
   C) Bucky Harris
   D) Gene Michael

5) Who is the only Yankees pitcher to throw more than one no-hitter?

    A)   Allie Reynolds
    B)   Dwight Gooden
    C)   Dave Righetti
    D)   Jim Abbott

6) Which of the following positions is not represented by a Yankee in the National Baseball Hall of Fame?

    A)   Left Fielder
    B)   Short Stop
    C)   Third Baseman
    D)   Catcher

7) What is the highest career winning percentage of a Yankees pitcher (minimum 100 decisions)?

    A)   .653
    B)   .717
    C)   .790
    D)   .822

8) Who was the first-ever non-New York team the Yankees faced in the World Series?

    A)   Cincinnati Reds
    B)   St. Louis Cardinals
    C)   Chicago Cubs
    D)   Milwaukee Brewers

9) Against which AL opponent does New York have the lowest all-time regular-season winning percentage?

A) Detroit Tigers
B) Cleveland Indians
C) Boston Red Sox
D) Chicago White Sox

10) Who is the only Yankees manager to have his jersey number retired?

A) Ralph Houk
B) Joe McCarthy
C) Miller Huggins
D) Casey Stengel

11) Against which team did Derek Jeter get hit number 2,722 to become the Yankees all-time hit leader?

A) Baltimore Orioles
B) Tampa Bay Rays
C) Detroit Tigers
D) Los Angeles Angels of Anaheim

12) Which Yankees manager had the highest winning percentage in postseason play?

A) Joe Torre
B) Casey Stengel
C) Joe McCarthy
D) Miller Huggins

13) What are the most errors the Yankees have committed in a single season?

    A) 159
    B) 211
    C) 260
    D) 386

14) Which Yankees pitcher did not win a Gold Glove?

    A) Bobby Shantz
    B) Andy Pettitte
    C) Mike Mussina
    D) Ron Guidry

15) Which New York manager had the highest winning percentage (minimum 3 seasons)?

    A) Joe McCarthy
    B) Billy Martin
    C) Joe Torre
    D) Yogi Berra

16) How many Yankees have recorded over 250 stolen bases?

    A) 1
    B) 3
    C) 4
    D) 6

17) Who was the most recent Yankees player to be named American League Home Run Champion?

    A)   Bernie Williams
    B)   Jason Giambi
    C)   Mark Teixeira
    D)   Alex Rodriguez

18) What are the most home runs Derek Jeter has hit in a season with the Yankees?

    A)   18
    B)   24
    C)   31
    D)   37

19) When was the last time the leading player for the Yankees had fewer than 100 RBIs?

    A)   1962
    B)   1976
    C)   1983
    D)   1995

20) What is the current distance to the center field wall at Yankee Stadium?

    A)   389'
    B)   408'
    C)   420'
    D)   455'

21) Who was the most recent Yankees starting pitcher to lead the team in strikeouts, wins, innings pitched, and ERA in the same season?

   A) Randy Johnson
   B) Roger Clemens
   C) CC Sabathia
   D) David Cone

22) How many all-time team captains has New York had?

   A) 8
   B) 11
   C) 14
   D) 17

23) Mariano Rivera's jersey number was retired by the Yankees in 1997.

   A) True
   B) False

24) When was the last time the Yankees had a team batting average of .300 or higher?

   A) 1936
   B) 1957
   C) 1961
   D) 1976

25) Did Babe Ruth end his career with the Yankees?

   A) Yes
   B) No

26) Who was the first-ever Yankee to lead the league in hits?

   A) Earl Combs
   B) Lou Gehrig
   C) Joe DiMaggio
   D) Phil Rizzuto

27) What is the largest-ever deficit overcome in a Yankees victory?

   A) 6 points
   B) 8 points
   C) 9 points
   D) 11 points

28) Who did the Yankees play on opening day in 2009?

   A) Toronto Blue Jays
   B) Detroit Tigers
   C) Tampa Bay Rays
   D) Baltimore Orioles

29) Mariano Rivera has twice as many career saves with the Yankees as Dave Righetti.

A) True
B) False

30) What is the combined winning percentage of New York mangers who lasted one season or less?

A) .468
B) .480
C) .506
D) .543

31) What famous college football game was held at Yankee Stadium in 1928?

A) Army-Navy
B) Harvard-Yale
C) Michigan-Ohio State
D) Notre Dame-Army

32) What are the most consecutive losses the Yankees have ever had in one season?

A) 6
B) 9
C) 13
D) 15

33) How many home runs did Babe Ruth and Reggie Jackson hit to set the major league record for home runs in a World Series game?

    A) 2
    B) 3
    C) 4
    D) 5

34) What are the Yankees' fewest-ever losses in one season?

    A) 21
    B) 34
    C) 44
    D) 48

35) The only time the Yankees had two players with greater than 50 home runs in the same season was 1961.

    A) True
    B) False

36) Which player holds the Yankees' record for most games in a season with an at-bat?

    A) Lou Gehrig
    B) Mickey Mantle
    C) Derek Jeter
    D) Hideki Matsui

37) Who was New York's first round draft pick in 2009?

    A) Caleb Cotham
    B) Slade Heathcott
    C) Adam Warren
    D) J.R. Murphy

38) Who holds the Yankees' record for runs scored in a career?

    A) Babe Ruth
    B) Derek Jeter
    C) Yogi Berra
    D) Joe DiMaggio

39) What are the most home runs in a season by a Yankees pitcher?

    A) 5
    B) 12
    C) 15
    D) 21

40) When was the last time the leading hitter for the Yankees had a batting average below .300?

    A) 1963
    B) 1980
    C) 1991
    D) 2004

41) Who is the only Yankees pitcher to win the AL Triple Crown (led the league in ERA, wins, and strikeouts)?

    A) Roger Clemens
    B) Lefty Gomez
    C) Mariano Rivera
    D) Whitey Ford

42) What is the Yankees' record for most innings played in a single game?

    A) 15
    B) 18
    C) 22
    D) 25

43) What position did Yankees manager Joe Girardi play?

    A) Center Fielder
    B) Shortstop
    C) Second Baseman
    D) Catcher

44) Who hit the walk-off home run in game seven of the ALCS against Boston in 2003?

    A) Derek Jeter
    B) Aaron Boone
    C) Jason Giambi
    D) Jorge Posada

45) What is the nickname of the group of fans occupying section 203 at Yankee Stadium?

A) Yankee Crazies
B) Diamond Drones
C) Ruth's Brutes
D) Bleacher Creatures

46) What color are the letters that spell "Yankee Stadium" over the main gate entrance?

A) Blue
B) White
C) Black
D) White with Pinstripes

47) Which of the following Yankees players was born in Panama?

A) Mariano Rivera
B) Jorge Posada
C) Melky Cabrera
D) Jose Molina

48) Since 1921, what is New York's longest drought between American League Pennants?

A) 7 years
B) 12 years
C) 14 years
D) 19 years

49) Did the Yankees have a better batting average against right-handed pitchers than left-handed pitchers in 2009?

   A) Yes
   B) No

50) Since 1923, what is New York's longest drought between World Series wins?

   A) 6 years
   B) 9 years
   C) 12 years
   D) 17 years

Cool Fact

Yankee Stadium has always had much to offer fans – excitement, tradition, championships, and… very large scoreboards. The first scoreboard in 1923 was large enough to show 12 innings of action for every major league baseball game. In 1959 a scoreboard with "message technology" was installed and was billed as the world's largest scoreboard. However, even this was not big enough. In 1974 another scoreboard with a length of 560 feet was unveiled. It was baseball's first-ever "telescreen" and had the innovative technology to show instant replays.

1) A – 1 (Jeter hit his first and only grand slam for the Yankees against the Cubs on June 18, 2005. This was his 136th career at-bat with the bases loaded.)

2) C – Jorge Posada (He hit a solo home run in the fifth inning off of Cleveland pitcher Cliff Lee in the first game at the new stadium.)

3) D – 1992 (The Yankees finished 76-86 [.469].)

4) A – Casey Stengel (Casey won 1,149 games as a Yankees manager.)

5) A – Allie Reynolds (Allie threw two no-hitters in 1951 and is one of only four pitchers to throw two no-hitters in the same season.)

6) C – Third Baseman (All other positions are represented with at least one Yankee in the Hall of Fame.)

7) B – .717 (Spud Chandler went 109-43 from 1937-47.)

8) B – St. Louis Cardinals (The Yankees faced the New York Giants in their first three World Series match-ups before playing the Cardinals in 1926. The Yankees lost the series 3-4.)

9) A – Detroit Tigers (The Yankees are 1,016-899, for a .531 winning percentage against the Tigers.)

10) D – Casey Stengel (He had his jersey number [#37] retired in 1970. Billy Martin is included as a player, even though he managed NY, due to his integral role in the World Championships of the 1950s.)

11) A – Baltimore Orioles (Jeter passed Lou Gehrig as the Yankees all-time hit leader with a single off of Orioles pitcher Chris Tillman on Sept. 11, 2009.)

12) C – Joe McCarthy (Joe led the Yankees to an astounding 29-9 [.763] record in postseason play, winning eight pennants and seven World Series titles.)

13) D – 386 (1912)

14) B – Andy Pettitte (Bobby Shantz won four Gold Gloves [1957-60], Ron Guidry won five [1982-86], and Mike Mussina won three [2001, 2003, and 2008].)

15) A – Joe McCarthy (Joe had an overall record of 1,460-867, for a .627 winning percentage as a Yankees manager.)

16) B – 3 (Rickey Henderson [326], Derek Jeter [305], and Willie Randolph [251])

17) C – Mark Teixeira (Mark last won this award in 2009 with 39 home runs, the first of his career.)

18) B – 24 (Jeter hit 24 home runs in 1999.)

19) D – 1995 (Paul O'Neil led the Yankees with 96 RBIs.)

20) B – 408' (The dimensions of the current Yankee Stadium are the same as the original Yankee Stadium.)

21) C – CC Sabathia (In 2009 Sabathia had 197 strikeouts, 19 wins, 230.0 innings pitched, and had a 3.37 ERA.)

22) B – 11 (Hal Chase, Roger Peckinpaugh, Babe Ruth [even though he only captained for six days], Everett Scott, Lou Gehrig, Thurman Munson, Graig Nettles, Willie Randolph, Ron Guidry, Don Mattingly, and Derek Jeter)

23) A – True (Jackie Robinson's jersey number was retired by every major league team in 1997. Mariano will be the last Yankee to wear number 42.)

24) A – 1936 (This has happened only 4 times in Yankees history [.300 in 1921, .307 in 1927, .309 in 1930, and .300 in 1936].)

25) B – No (Babe was traded to the Boston Braves in 1935 where he played one last season before retiring.)

26) A – Earl Combs (He led the league with 231 hits in 1927.)

27) C – 9 points (This happened three times, the last one against the Rangers in 2006 to win 14-13.)

28) D – Baltimore Orioles (The Yankees lost 5-10 to the Orioles.)

29) A – True (Rivera has 526 career saves with the Yankees and Dave Righetti is second with 224.)

30) B – .480 (Yankees managers who lasted one season or less had a combined record of 432-468, for a .480 winning percentage.)

31) D – Notre Dame-Army (The Fighting Irish went on to defeat the Cadets 12-6 after Knute Rockne's famous halftime "win one for the Gipper" speech.)

32) C – 13 (The Yankees lost every game from May 21 to June 6 of the 1913 season.)

33) B – 3 (Jackson hit three in Game Six of the 1977 World Series and Ruth hit three in Game Four of both the 1926 and 1928 World Series.)

34) C – 44 (In 1927 the Yankees finished 110-44.)

35) A – True (Roger Maris had 61 and Mickey Mantle had 54.)

36) D – Hideki Matsui (163 games in 2003)

37) B – Slade Heathcott (Heathcott is a 6'1" CF out of Texas High School in Texarkana, Texas. He was the 29th pick in the first round.)

38) A – Babe Ruth (1,959 career runs scored)

39) A – 5 (Red Ruffing, 1936)

40) D – 2004 (Hideki Matsui led the Yankees with a .298 batting average.)

41) B – Lefty Gomez (He won the Triple Crown in 1934 [2.33 ERA, 26 wins, and 158 strikeouts] and again in 1937 [2.33 ERA, 21 wins, and 194 strikeouts].)

42) C – 22 (In 1962 the Yankees pulled out a 9-7 win over Detroit after 22 innings of play.)

43) D – Catcher (Girardi played professional baseball from 1989-2003 with the Cubs, Rockies, Yankees, and Cardinals.)

44) B – Aaron Boone (He hit a solo home run in the bottom of the 11th against Tim Wakefield.)

45) D – Bleacher Creatures (These fanatical fans do a "roll call" of Yankees players and have various songs and chants [sometimes vulgar].)

46) A – Blue (The letters were originally white but were painted blue in the 1960s.)

47) A – Mariano Rivera (He was born in Panama City, Panama. The Yankees had 14 internationally born players on the roster in 2009.)

48) C – 14 years (The Yankees did not win an AL Pennant from 1982-95.)

49) B – No (The Yankees batted .282 against right-handed pitchers and .286 against left-handed pitchers.)

50) D – 17 years (The Yankees did not win a World Series from 1979-95.)

Note: All answers valid as of the end of the 2009 season, unless otherwise indicated in the question itself.

1) Which of the following managers has not been inducted into the National Baseball Hall of Fame as a Yankee?

Answers begin on page 75

    A) Joe McCarthy
    B) Miller Huggins
    C) Casey Stengel
    D) Ralph Houk

2) Who was the first-ever African-American player to play for the Yankees?

    A) Elston Howard
    B) Moises Alou
    C) Reggie Jackson
    D) Dave Winfield

3) What song is played at Yankee Stadium following a home game?

    A) "We Are the Champions"
    B) "New York, New York"
    C) "Take Me Out to the Ballgame"
    D) "America the Beautiful"

4) Where is the Yankees' Latin Beisbol Academy located?

    A) Mexico
    B) Honduras
    C) Dominican Republic
    D) Puerto Rico

5) Did Babe Ruth ever pitch for the Yankees?

    A) Yes
    B) No

6) Why did Joe DiMaggio not play with the Yankees from 1943-45?

    A) Injured
    B) Joined the Army
    C) Traded to Detroit
    D) Retired from Baseball

7) What are the most consecutive winning seasons the Yankees have ever had?

    A) 12
    B) 19
    C) 25
    D) 39

8) How many teams has New York played greater than 2,000 times in the regular season?

    A) 2
    B) 3
    C) 4
    D) 6

9) How many games did the Yankees win in 2009 when trailing going into the ninth inning?

   A) 1
   B) 5
   C) 11
   D) 14

10) Which Yankees player won the most Gold Gloves?

   A) Bobby Richardson
   B) Joe Pepitone
   C) Dave Winfield
   D) Don Mattingly

11) What team did Joe Girardi manage before the Yankees?

   A) Florida Marlins
   B) Atlanta Braves
   C) Milwaukee Brewers
   D) Houston Astros

12) Which Yankee led the league in runs in a single season the greatest number of times?

   A) Rickey Henderson
   B) Mickey Mantle
   C) Babe Ruth
   D) Lou Gehrig

13) Which of the following Yankees players never had a batting average over .375 for a single season?

   A)   Babe Ruth
   B)   Joe DiMaggio
   C)   Lou Gehrig
   D)   Mickey Mantle

14) How many times was Billy Martin the Yankees' manager?

   A)   1
   B)   3
   C)   5
   D)   6

15) What year did a group headed by George Steinbrenner purchase the Yankees?

   A)   1971
   B)   1973
   C)   1976
   D)   1981

16) The scoreboard at Yankee Stadium is over 5,000 square feet.

   A)   True
   B)   False

17) How many Yankees batters have won the American League Triple Crown?

    A) 1
    B) 2
    C) 4
    D) 5

18) When was the last time the Yankees failed to hit 100 or more home runs in a season?

    A) 1971
    B) 1976
    C) 1982
    D) 1985

19) Where do the Yankees hold spring training?

    A) Greensboro, N.C.
    B) Lexington, Ky.
    C) Tampa, Fla.
    D) Savannah, Ga.

20) Who is the only Yankees pitcher to lead the team in strikeouts for five consecutive seasons?

    A) David Cone
    B) Bob Turley
    C) Jack Chesbro
    D) Ron Guidry

21) All-time, how many managers have the Yankees had?

   A) 21
   B) 26
   C) 32
   D) 37

22) Who threw out the ceremonial first pitch for the first-ever game at the current Yankee Stadium?

   A) Barrack Obama
   B) Yogi Berra
   C) David Paterson
   D) Don Mattingly

23) Which Yankees manager has the second highest career winning percentage (minimum three seasons)?

   A) Billy Martin
   B) Miller Huggins
   C) Joe Torre
   D) Casey Stengel

24) Do the Yankees have a winning record in the regular season against National League teams?

   A) Yes
   B) No

25) What are the most times a Yankees player has been hit by pitch in a season?

A) 23
B) 31
C) 35
D) 40

26) What year did the Yankees play a tie game in the World Series?

A) 1922
B) 1927
C) 1932
D) 1943

27) What year was the Yankees' first-ever home night game?

A) 1933
B) 1939
C) 1946
D) 1950

28) Which of the following players was not a lead-off batter for the Yankees in 2009?

A) Johnny Damon
B) Derek Jeter
C) Brett Gardner
D) Nick Swisher

29) What decade did the Yankees have the lowest winning percentage?

    A)   1900s
    B)   1910s
    C)   1970s
    D)   1980s

30) The Yankees attendance more than doubled the first season Babe Ruth played for them.

    A)   True
    B)   False

31) How many seasons have the Yankees finished in first place then failed to win the World Series?

    A)   12
    B)   15
    C)   18
    D)   22

32) What is the lowest team batting average the Yankees had in a single season?

    A)   .196
    B)   .214
    C)   .225
    D)   .237

33) Which pitcher holds the Yankees' career record for most
strikeouts?

    A)   Mariano Rivera
    B)   Ron Guidry
    C)   Whitey Ford
    D)   Red Ruffing

34) What are the most home wins the Yankees had in a
single season?

    A) 56
    B) 59
    C) 62
    D) 65

35) Who was the most recent Yankee to win American
League Rookie of the Year?

    A)   Derek Jeter
    B)   Thurman Munson
    C)   Dave Righetti
    D)   Tony Kubek

36) How many times has New York lost a postseason
divisional series?

    A) 2
    B) 4
    C) 6
    D) 7

37) How many times have the Yankees swept the opposing team in the World Series?

    A) 3
    B) 5
    C) 6
    D) 8

38) What was the lowest regular-season winning percentage of a Yankees World Series Championship team?

    A) .540
    B) .588
    C) .614
    D) .679

39) Which National League team have the Yankees played the greatest number of times during the regular season?

    A) New York Mets
    B) San Francisco Giants
    C) Milwaukee Brewers
    D) Washington Nationals

40) Has Mariano Rivera ever had a hit for the Yankees?

    A) Yes
    B) No

41) What is the nickname of the Yankees' single A affiliate located in Charleston, S.C.?

    A) Grasshoppers
    B) Chasers
    C) Legends
    D) RiverDogs

42) Who was the most recent Yankee to lead MLB in batting average?

    A) Paul O'Neil
    B) Bernie Williams
    C) Derek Jeter
    D) Alex Rodriguez

43) How many consecutive games did Lou Gehrig play in his career as a Yankee?

    A) 2,130
    B) 2,260
    C) 2,371
    D) 2,390

44) What was the highest winning percentage by a Yankees manager who lasted one season or less?

    A) .421
    B) .508
    C) .583
    D) .632

45) When was the last time the Yankees failed to score 750 runs in a season?

    A) 1975
    B) 1987
    C) 1995
    D) 2003

46) Which Yankees player holds the American League record for most RBIs in a single game?

    A) Tony Lazzeri
    B) Babe Ruth
    C) Reggie Jackson
    D) Lou Gehrig

47) Including perfect games, how many no-hitters have been thrown by Yankees pitchers?

    A) 5
    B) 7
    C) 9
    D) 11

48) How many times have the Yankees won 100 or more games in a season without winning the World Series?

    A) 2
    B) 4
    C) 7
    D) 9

49) What is the Yankees' all-time record for consecutive wins?

    A) 15
    B) 19
    C) 22
    D) 24

50) Which Yankees great holds the team record for career hits in the World Series?

    A) Babe Ruth
    B) Mickey Mantle
    C) Lou Gehrig
    D) Yogi Berra

Lou Gehrig showed athletic ability in baseball and football early on. For example, once in a high school game his senior year he hit a grand slam in the ninth inning at Wrigley Field. In 1921 he left home to attend Columbia University on a football scholarship. Before the first semester even began he was swayed by the New York Giants manager to play minor league baseball with the Hartford Senators. Risking his football scholarship, Gehrig changed his name to Henry Lewis, but was later discovered and banned from intercollegiate play his freshman year. The following year he was allowed to suit up as a fullback for the Columbia Lions. However, it was not too long before Gehrig's true calling rose above all other competing interests. He began playing baseball for Columbia his sophomore year and had a .444 batting average. Gehrig also struck out 17 batters in a game he pitched for the Lions – a single-game record at Columbia to this day. Soon after he was signed by the Yankees and history was made.

Yankeeology Trivia Challenge

1) D – Ralph Houk (Joe McCarthy was inducted in 1957, Miller Huggins in 1964, and Casey Stengel in 1966.)

2) A – Elston Howard (Elston made the club in 1955. He went on to win two Gold Gloves and the AL MVP in 1963. His jersey number was retired by the Yankees in 1984.)

3) B – "New York, New York" ([The Frank Sinatra version] At one time the Liza Minnelli version was played after a loss.)

4) C – Dominican Republic (New York uses this training academy to help develop Latin American players.)

5) A – Yes (Ruth pitched a total of 5 games going 5-0. He only gave up one home run in 31 innings pitched.)

6) B – Joined the Army (Joe served 31 months in the Army, and rose to the rank of Sergeant.)

7) D – 39 (1926-64)

8) A – 2 (The Yankees have played Baltimore 2,021 times in the regular season and Boston 2,012 times.)

9) B – 5 (The Yankees were 5-53 [.086] when down and heading into the ninth inning.)

10) D – Don Mattingly (Donnie Baseball won 9 Gold Gloves [1985-89, 1991-94].)

11) A – Florida Marlins (Girardi won NL Manager of the Year in 2006 after just his first year as a manager with the Florida Marlins.)

12) C – Babe Ruth (7 times: 1920 [158], 1921 [177], 1923 [151], 1924 [143], 1926 [139], 1927 [158], and 1928 [163])

13) D – Mickey Mantle (Mantle's highest average was .365 in 1957 [Ruth .393 in 1923, DiMaggio .381 in 1939, and Gehrig .379 in 1930].)

14) C – 5 ([1975-78, 1979, 1983, 1985, and 1988] This is a major league record for the most times managing one team.)

15) B – 1973 (Steinbrenner's group bought the Yankees from CBS for $10 million after New York failed to win a pennant for eight straight seasons.)

16) A – True (The new scoreboard is 59' tall by 101' wide for a total of 5,959 square feet.)

17) B – 2 (Lou Gehrig in 1934 [49 home runs, 165 RBIs, and .363 batting average] and Mickey Mantle in 1956 [52 home runs, 130 RBIs, & .353 batting average])

18) A – 1971 (The Yankees hit 97 home runs as a team.)

19) C – Tampa, Fla. (The Yankees hold spring training at their Advanced A affiliate facility – the Tampa Yankees' Steinbrenner Field.)

20) D – Ron Guidry (1977 [176], 1978 [248], 1979 [201], 1980 [166], and 1981 [104])

21) C – 32 (From Clark Griffith to Joe Girardi)

22) B – Yogi Berra (The Yankee great was 83 years old.)

23) D – Casey Stengel (The Yankees had an overall record of 1,149-696 under Stengel, for a .623 winning percentage.)

24) A – Yes (340-275 for a .553 winning percentage)

25) A – 23 (Ben Chapman in 1931)

26) A – 1922 (The Yankees played to a 3-3 tie with the Giants before the game was called due to darkness. The Giants won the series 4-0.)

27) C – 1946 (The Yankees beat the Washington Senators 2-1 under the lights on May 28. Lights were installed at the stadium in 1946.)

28) D – Nick Swisher (Jeter was the lead-off batter for 147 games, Brett Gardner for 11 games, and Johnny Damon for four games.)

29) B – 1910s (The Yankees had an overall record of 701-780 for a winning percentage of .473. The only decade NY finished under .500.)

30) A – True (Attendance went from just over 619,000 to over 1,289,000.)

31) C – 18 (Does not include 1994 when the World Series was cancelled due to a strike.)

32) B – .214 (NY hit 1,137 for 5,310 as a team in 1968.)

33) C – Whitey Ford (1,956 strikeouts in 16 seasons)

34) D – 65 (NY finished 65-16 at home in 1961.)

35) A – Derek Jeter (He won this award in 1996. Other winners are Gil McDougald [1951], Tony Kubek [1957], Tom Tresh [1962], and Thurman Munson [1970]. The following won as pitchers: Bob Grim [1954], Stan Bahnsen [1968], and Dave Righetti [1981].)

36) C – 6 (NY lost to the Mariners in 1995 [2-3], Indians in 1997 [2-3] and 2007 [1-3], Angels in 2002 [1-3] and 2005 [2-3], and the Tigers in 2006 [1-3].)

37) D – 8 (Pirates [1927], Cardinals [1928], Cubs [1932 and 1938], Reds [1939], Phillies [1950], Padres [1998], and Braves [1999])

38) A – .540 (In 2000 the Yankees finished 87-74 before moving on to beat the Mets 4-1 in the World Series.)

39) C – Milwaukee Brewers (The Yankees have played the Brewers 390 times for a 208-182 [.533] record. The Brewers were part of the AL before moving to the NL in 1998.)

40) B – No (Mariano has only had three career plate appearances during the regular season, resulting in no hits.)

41) D – RiverDogs ([Of the Southern division of the South Atlantic League] The RiverDogs have been affiliated with the Yankees since 2005.)

42) B – Bernie Williams (In 1998 Bernie led the league with a .339 batting average.)

43) A – 2,130 (The "Iron Horse" began his streak of 2,130 consecutive games played on June 1, 1925 and it ended on May 30, 1939. This record lasted 56 years until broken by Cal Ripken in 1995.)

44) D – .632 (Dick Howser managed the Yankees to a 103-60 record in the 1980 regular season. NY went to the postseason, getting swept 0-3 by Kansas City.)

45) C – 1995 (The Yankees scored 749 runs and finished 79-65 in Buck Showalter's last season as manager.)

46) A – Tony Lazzeri (Tony hit 11 RBIs against the Philadelphia Athletics on May 24, 1936 [Yankees 25, Athletics 2].)

47) D – 11 (George Mogridge in 1917, Sam Jones in 1923, Monte Pearson in 1928, Allie Reynolds twice in 1951, Dave Righetti in 1983, Jim Abbott in 1993, and Dwight Gooden in 1996 [includes perfect games by Cone, Well, and Larson].)

48) C – 7 (1942, 1954, 1963, 1980, and 2002-04)

49) B – 19 (New York won 19 consecutive games in 1947.)

50) D – Yogi Berra (He recorded 71 hits in 75 World Series games with the Yankees.)

Note: All answers valid as of the end of the 2009 season, unless otherwise indicated in the question itself.

1) How many Yankees managers have won at least one World Series?

Answers begin on page 83

   A) 5
   B) 7
   C) 9
   D) 11

2) What is the only decade, since the 1920s, that the Yankees failed to wi a World Series?

   A) 1940s
   B) 1960s
   C) 1970s
   D) 1980s

3) How many overall no.-1 draft picks have the Yankees had?

   A) 0
   B) 2
   C) 4
   D) 5

4) Which Yankees pitcher had the most wild pitches in 2009?

   A) Joba Chamberlain
   B) CC Sabathia
   C) A.J. Burnett
   D) Phil Coke

5) What are the most wins by a Yankees pitcher in a single season?

    A) 24
    B) 29
    C) 35
    D) 41

6) What was Yankee great Babe Ruth's real name?

    A) George Herman
    B) Andrew Long
    C) Jacob Johenson
    D) Harold Kelley

7) How many times has New York finished the regular season in first place?

    A) 34
    B) 37
    C) 41
    D) 45

8) New York has more pitchers than outfielders enshrined in the National Baseball Hall of Fame.

    A) True
    B) False

9) Who is the only Yankees pitcher to be a unanimous selection for the Cy Young Award?

   A) Whitey Ford
   B) Bob Turley
   C) Ron Guidry
   D) Roger Clemens

10) What are the most runs scored by the Yankees in a nine-inning game?

   A) 25
   B) 27
   C) 29
   D) 31

1) C – 9 (McCarthy and Stengel [7], Torre [4], Huggins [3], Houk [2], Martin, Harris, Lemon, and Girardi [1])

2) D – 1980s (NY only had one World Series appearance in the decade [1981].)

3) B – 2 (The Yankees drafted LHP Brien Taylor No. 1 in 1991 and first baseman Ron Blomberg in 1967.)

4) C – A.J. Burnett (He led the team with 17 wild pitches.)

5) D – 41 (Jack Chesbro went 41-12 in 1904.)

6) A – George Herman (Born in Baltimore, Md. in 1895, the Babe passed away in 1948, 13 years after his retirement from baseball.)

7) D – 45 (The last time was in 2009.)

8) A – True (Seven pitchers [Jack Chesbro, Herb Pennock, Red Ruffing, Waite Hoyt, Whitey Ford, Lefty Gomez, and Rich Gossage] and six outfielders [Babe Ruth, Willie Keeler, Joe DiMaggio, Earl Combs, Mickey Mantle, and Dave Winfield])

9) C – Ron Guidry (Ron was a unanimous selection in 1978 with a 25-3 record and 1.74 ERA.)

10) A – 25 (NY beat the Philadelphia Athletics 25-2 in 1936.)

Note: All answers valid as of the end of the 2009 season, unless otherwise indicated in the question itself.

Player / Team Score Sheet

Name:_____

Spring Training		Regular Season		Postseason		Championship Series		Extra Innings Bonus	
1	26	1	26	1	26	1	26	1	
2	27	2	27	2	27	2	27	2	
3	28	3	28	3	28	3	28	3	
4	29	4	29	4	29	4	29	4	
5	30	5	30	5	30	5	30	5	
6	31	6	31	6	31	6	31	6	
7	32	7	32	7	32	7	32	7	
8	33	8	33	8	33	8	33	8	
9	34	9	34	9	34	9	34	9	
10	35	10	35	10	35	10	35	10	
11	36	11	36	11	36	11	36		
12	37	12	37	12	37	12	37		
13	38	13	38	13	38	13	38		
14	39	14	39	14	39	14	39		
15	40	15	40	15	40	15	40		
16	41	16	41	16	41	16	41		
17	42	17	42	17	42	17	42		
18	43	18	43	18	43	18	43		
19	44	19	44	19	44	19	44		
20	45	20	45	20	45	20	45		
21	46	21	46	21	46	21	46		
22	47	22	47	22	47	22	47		
23	48	23	48	23	48	23	48		
24	49	24	49	24	49	24	49		
25	50	25	50	25	50	25	50		

___x 1 =_____   ___x 2 =_____   ___x 3 =_____   ___x 4 =_____   ___x 4 =_____

Multiply total number correct by point value/quarter to calculate totals for each quarter.

Add total of all quarters below.

Total Points:_____

Thank you for playing *Yankeeology Trivia Challenge*.

Additional score sheets are available at:
www.TriviaGameBooks.com

Player / Team Score Sheet

Name:_____

Spring Training		Regular Season		Postseason		Championship Series		Extra Innings Bonus	
1	26	1	26	1	26	1	26	1	
2	27	2	27	2	27	2	27	2	
3	28	3	28	3	28	3	28	3	
4	29	4	29	4	29	4	29	4	
5	30	5	30	5	30	5	30	5	
6	31	6	31	6	31	6	31	6	
7	32	7	32	7	32	7	32	7	
8	33	8	33	8	33	8	33	8	
9	34	9	34	9	34	9	34	9	
10	35	10	35	10	35	10	35	10	
11	36	11	36	11	36	11	36		
12	37	12	37	12	37	12	37		
13	38	13	38	13	38	13	38		
14	39	14	39	14	39	14	39		
15	40	15	40	15	40	15	40		
16	41	16	41	16	41	16	41		
17	42	17	42	17	42	17	42		
18	43	18	43	18	43	18	43		
19	44	19	44	19	44	19	44		
20	45	20	45	20	45	20	45		
21	46	21	46	21	46	21	46		
22	47	22	47	22	47	22	47		
23	48	23	48	23	48	23	48		
24	49	24	49	24	49	24	49		
25	50	25	50	25	50	25	50		
___ x 1 =____		___ x 2 =____		___ x 3 =____		___ x 4 =____		___ x 4 =____	

Multiply total number correct by point value/quarter to calculate totals for each quarter.

Add total of all quarters below.

Total Points:_____

Thank you for playing *Yankeeology Trivia Challenge*.

Additional score sheets are available at:
www.TriviaGameBooks.com